# THE CAT OWNER'S HANDBOOK

BY MARCUS SCHNECK & JILL CARAVAN

NEW BURLINGTON BOOKS

A QUINTET BOOK



ISBN: 1-85348-722-8

This book was designed and produced by
Quintet Publishing Limited

Creative Director: Richard Dewing
Designer: Ian Hunt
Project Editor: Damien Thompson
Editor: Diana Vowles
Picture Researchers: Marcus Schneck and Jill Caravan
Jacket Design: Nik Morley

Typeset in Great Britain by
Central Southern Typesetters, Eastbourne
Manufactured in China by
Regent Publishing Services Limited.

Published by New Burlington Books
6, Blundell Street
London N7 9BH

# Contents

Perhaps it will be easier for you to accept your cat as an animal – albeit an animal that you love dearly and share your life with – if we first look at the history of the species.

The earliest known cat-like creatures emerged about 40 million years ago, about the same time as the earliest known dog-like creatures. At about this time in prehistory, the aeluroids (cat ancestors) and the arctoids (dog ancestors) went their separate ways from a common group of ancestors, known as miacids. The miacids, a group of small, arboreal carnivores, had been around for approximately 20 million years before that time.

In the above paragraph, you can find a very important point that will clarify a great deal about your cat. The ancestral line of our domestic cats,

**LEFT** *Cats are carnivores and predators. This doesn't make them "bad". It simply means that they have certain instincts and need certain things in their diet.*

**OPPOSITE** *The urge to hunt is instinctive, but the skills of the hunt and the kill are mostly learned. In today's world, many cats grow up never having received the full complement of those skills from their mothers.*

## The Ancestors of the Cat

**Dinictis** Existed until 40 million years ago. About the size of a lynx. Long upper canines used to stab prey.

**Pseudaelurus** These animals more closely resembled today's cats, with long limbs and five-toed feet. They began to die out 25 million years ago.

which some well-meaning people today are trying to convert to the kinder and gentler vegetarian lifestyle, traces directly from the very first modern carnivores. The cat who is now sleeping on the sofa next to you has been genetically programmed to eat meat for approximately 60 million years.

There are two ways for any creature to make its living as a meat-eater: hunt down prey and kill it, as carnivores generally do, or pick over the

**LEFT** *The domestic cats with which we share our lives and our homes are much more closely related to wild cats, including lions and tigers, than many cat owners imagine.*

remains of something that died of natural causes or was killed by some other creature, as scavengers do. Although they were never above scavenging when the opportunity presented itself, the ancestors of our cats generally followed the path of the hunter.

From their common aeluroid genus, cats gradually evolved into today's three genera: *Acinonyx*, the cheetah; *Panthera*, the great cats, such as lions and tigers; and *Felis*, the small cats, including our domestic cat and several small wild cats such as the ocelot and serval.

Along the evolutionary way, many experiments were tried but failed. For example, the sabre-toothed cat *Smilodon* was a top predator until about 13,000 years ago, when it ceased to exist. It was an evolutionary failure, probably because of the extinction of its prey species. Whatever the reason, none of the modern cats trace their lineage back to fearsome *Smilodon*.

So not only are our domestic cats the latest in a long line of hunters, they are the latest in a long line of hunters that were successful enough at hunting to survive and continue forward.

## CANINES AND FELINES – DIFFERENT HUNTERS

Modern-day canines such as domestic dogs, wolves, dingoes, foxes and the like have also found their way along the evolutionary path as hunters, although supplementing the meat they could kill with a much wider array of vegetable matter than any cat ever considered.

However, canines and felines found different ways to pursue the hunting life, and this is crucial to our understanding of our domestic dogs and cats today. The canines developed as group

**RIGHT** *You and your cat will be much more comfortable with one another if you are able to accept and respect his natural urges. They offer a learning experience for you and a comforting, secure environment for him.*

hunters, forming packs to work together in chasing down and killing their prey. The felines generally moved in the direction of the solitary hunter, relying on ambush and speed to take their prey.

There are, of course, exceptions to these rules. Some canines, such as the coyote of the western United States, more often hunt by themselves. (It's probably more than a coincidence that coyotes are excellent mousers and rely on rodents as a major portion of their diets.) Some felines, notably the lion, have chosen to live the group existence. (It's also interesting to note that the large, hoofed animals that the lions prey upon are rather similar to the principal prey species of canines such as the wolf.)

These hunting, and consequently lifestyle, "choices" made by long-gone ancestors are responsible for a large proportion of feline and canine behaviour today.

The pack lifestyle of the canine demands a highly socialized animal that acknowledges its subordinate standing to some members of its pack as well as its dominant standing over others. It relies on and supports all the other members of its pack. Group activities are the cornerstones of existence, as is a strong rule of order.

The lone-hunter lifestyle of the feline requires an independent animal that generally enforces its dominance over weaker animals and avoids stronger ones. Survival as a lone hunter is almost wholly dependent upon the abilities, skills and knowledge of the individual. Independent action and circumstance-based decisions are the cornerstones of existence.

Of course, man's interference in this natural progression – better known as domestication – has changed the situation somewhat. With the ample food and shelter that we provide for our cats, group interaction is more likely. This has occurred naturally in communities of feral cats that have gathered across the globe wherever man's garbage is collected or disposed of. It helps to explain the group behaviour that we often find in homes that have more than one cat, or even sometimes a cat and a dog. With all their needs fulfilled, the cat's instinctive behaviour patterns are more pliable.

Why shouldn't our cats "love" us? In return for them being there, for doing pretty much what they want to do anyway and for putting up with an occasional show of affection from us, we give them everything they need for life: food, water, shelter and protection. We even throw in some sense-heightening activity from time to time, such as dangling a bit of string for them to bat at or rolling a ball of yarn for the chase.

Love may be too human a word for it, but in the normal human-cat relationship there is a

**LEFT** *Deep attachments can form between cat and human, with each one bringing his or her own species' emotions and ways of showing them into the relationship.*

bond. It's not the same as the human-dog bond, which arises from the dog's pack instincts, nor is it the same as the human-horse bond, which arises from the human's mastery over the horse.

Cats are not pack animals. About the only time they can genuinely be described as naturally social animals is during their kittenhood. Yes, they do get together for courtship and mating (but add a third cat to that picture and you have anything but social behaviour!). And, yes, cats kept together as housemates will often display group activity. But that stems more from our treatment of them as lifelong kittens rather than from a real longing for life in a group.

All of this, however, does not negate the fact that a bond generally does exist between humans and their cats, or cats and their humans depending upon your perspective on the situation. In many ways we take the place of a parent figure, providing nearly all of the basic needs for our cats. This naturally leads to a certain amount of dependency on the part of the cat, although not nearly as much mental and emotional dependency as a dog would feel. At the same time, it leads us into a certain dependence on the cat for some of our well-being as well.

## Feline Affection

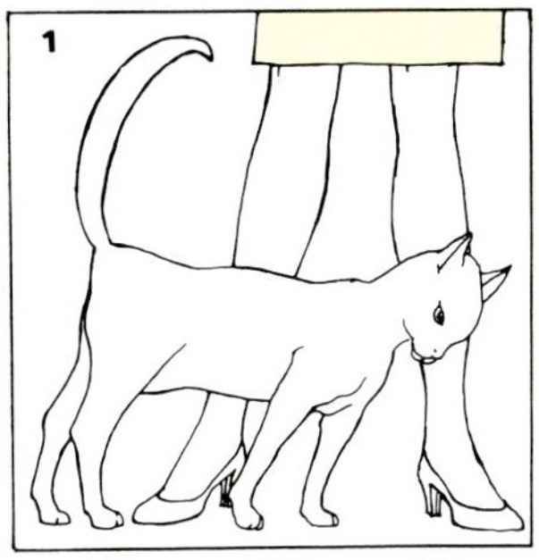

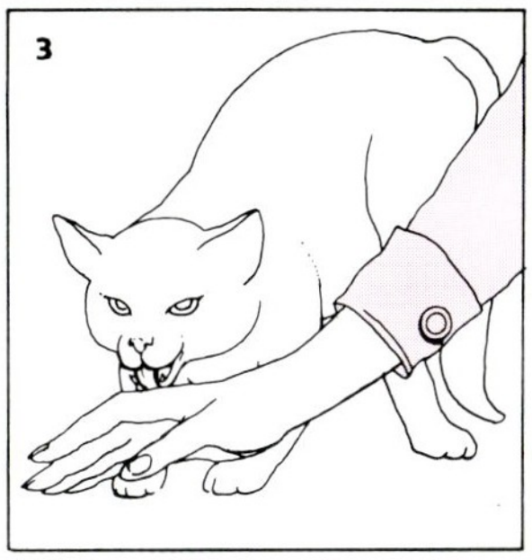


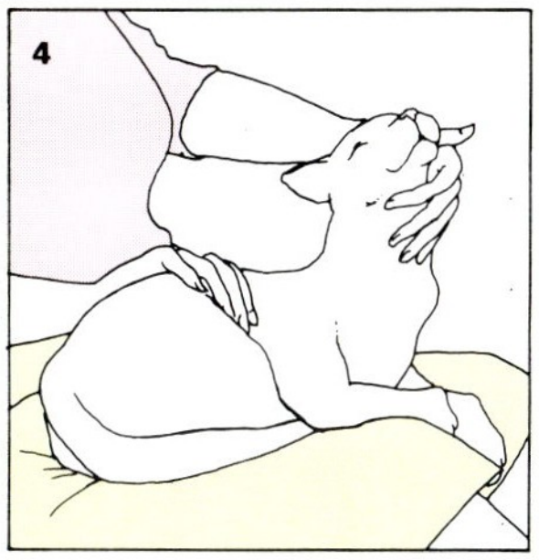


How do you politely introduce yourself? People shake hands, some dogs offer a paw. The really well-educated feline gently slides along human legs (1), maybe adding a gentle, purring vocal reminder of its arrival. Just in case you need a further message, a flaglike tail is raised in greeting. The message is clear and unmistakable – the cat wants to be introduced.

It takes a stern human to resist the attempts of the rubbing and licking cat to get itself picked up and petted (2). Another ploy is to lie on its back and look helpless. Once it has achieved its aim, the cat will continue to make contact. Sniffing a human's mouth or nose is a means of recognition and of saying "hello".

Man is always likely to take the poetry and romance out of anything. Some scientists insist that the reason cats lick human hands is to restore their deprived bodies with salt (3). Cat-lovers and less physiologically-minded students of behaviour believe that licking the hand is a mere preliminary to the much more obvious bond behaviours of mouth-to-mouth contact.

The lap is the cat's ultimate target (4). Some oriental types will not even give the human the option, but will simply leap on to a lap and settle down. The reason cats like lying on human laps is that they are comfortable and secure, and there can be few better reasons for doing anything.

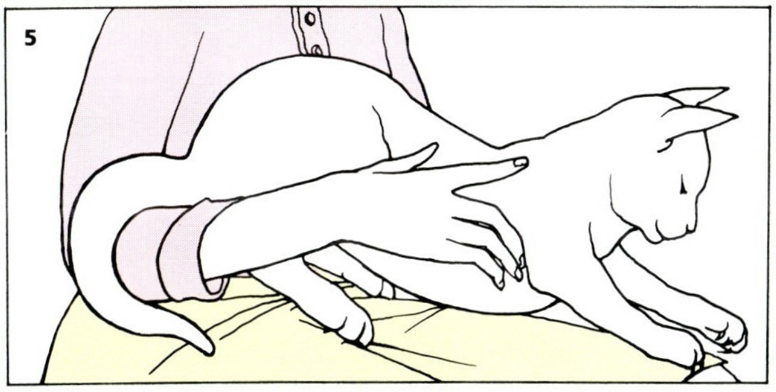


All cat-lovers have been on the receiving end of a gentle, but persistent pounding by paws (5). This is sometimes assisted, most uncomfortably, by claws, and always with the full strength of the cat's forelegs. This is the normal behaviour of the nursing kitten and it lingers on. Kittens deprived of that sort of behaviour in their early lives are much more likely to inflict it on their owners.

**LEFT** *Cats easily assimilate into the life of the household, to the extent that they allow themselves to join in. Some are more inclined to this than others.*

This is not a negative thing, unless that dependence becomes too strong for either party. A cat who spends nearly all of his time on his human's lap is probably too dependent – as is the human who forgoes activity outside the home to spend more time with his or her cat.

Let's insert one qualifier at this point. Cats are a popular companion for many homebound senior citizens. The links between these people and their cats are naturally going to be somewhat stronger and more intense than in many other human-cat relationships.

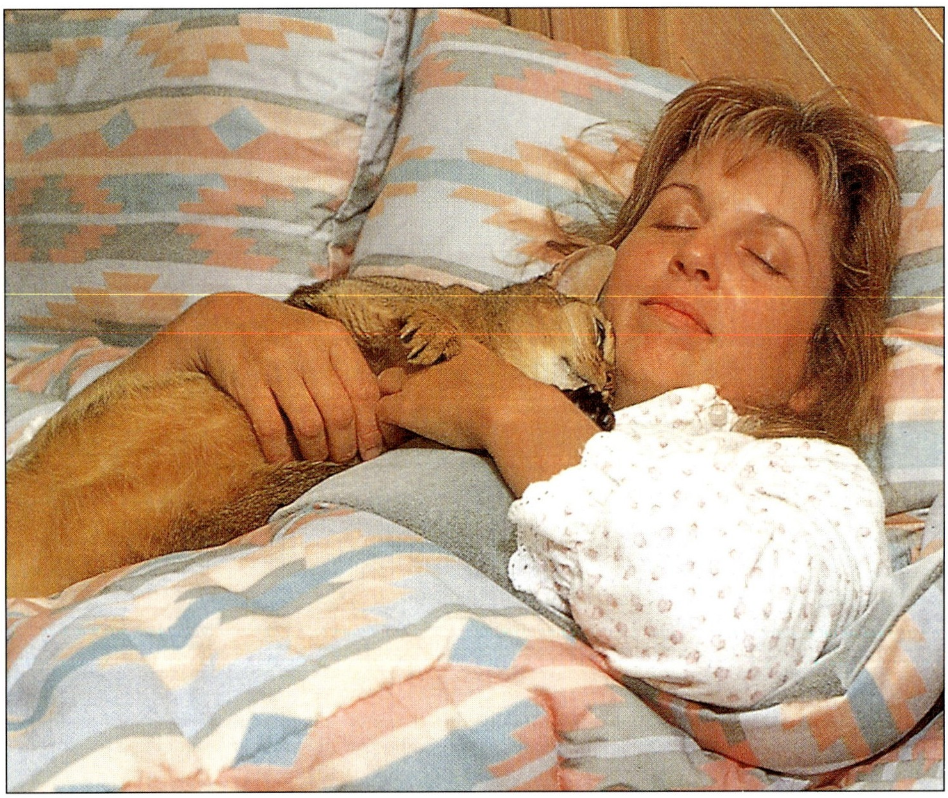

**LEFT** *Only a cat that is very comfortable in its relationship with a human would allow itself to be this exposed, even while asleep or almost asleep. Such chance-taking is the ultimate show of acceptance in the feline mind.*

**LEFT** *To forge better relationships with cats, children should be encouraged to view them as living things with their own needs and desires rather than warm and soft toys. Deep relationships can form if both parties are permitted naturally to be themselves.*

## CATS AND CHILDREN

At the other end of the age spectrum, cats can also develop warm relationships with children. Although dogs are the consummate baby-lovers, cats too can be wonderful around kids, from newborns to teenagers. With the exception of the occasional anti-social animal, a cat's attitude towards young humans is mostly determined by the initial human actions towards the cat.

When a newborn baby is brought into the home, the typical reaction by the parents and grandparents is to exclude the cat. How would you feel if you had suddenly been moved from one of the focal points in the home to a sideline position? All your attempts to garner attention that were previously seen as cute are now spurned and even discouraged. Is it any wonder that the cat soon comes to greet the new addition with a certain amount of resentment?

The solution is obvious. Include the cat in as much as possible that concerns the baby. Under close supervision, allow the cat to sniff the baby. When you're involved with the baby and the cat is nearby, be certain to mention the cat's name occasionally, offer it some praise and have some physical contact. Make sure that you're not cutting back too severely on playtime with the cat because of time spent with the baby.

The cat's relationship with children is to a large part determined by the approach that the humans adopt. Let's face the fact that children are noisy, rough and erratic. They get on our nerves, so why not our cats' nerves as well?

Pulling her tail, grabbing her ears, running at her, carrying her about like a doll are all guaranteed to put the cat off from further contact and so must be prevented. Children must also be taught that the cat is completely off-limits at certain times, primarily when she is eating, using the litter box or sleeping.

Many cat owners seem to assume that cats and children mix even less than oil and water. After a few negative experiences, they give up trying to introduce the cat to children on the basis that it seems best for everyone concerned simply to keep them apart. With just a bit of attention to

**RIGHT** *Cats are naturally curious about any addition to the home, especially a new baby. As long as adult supervision is constant, the cat poses no danger to the infant.*

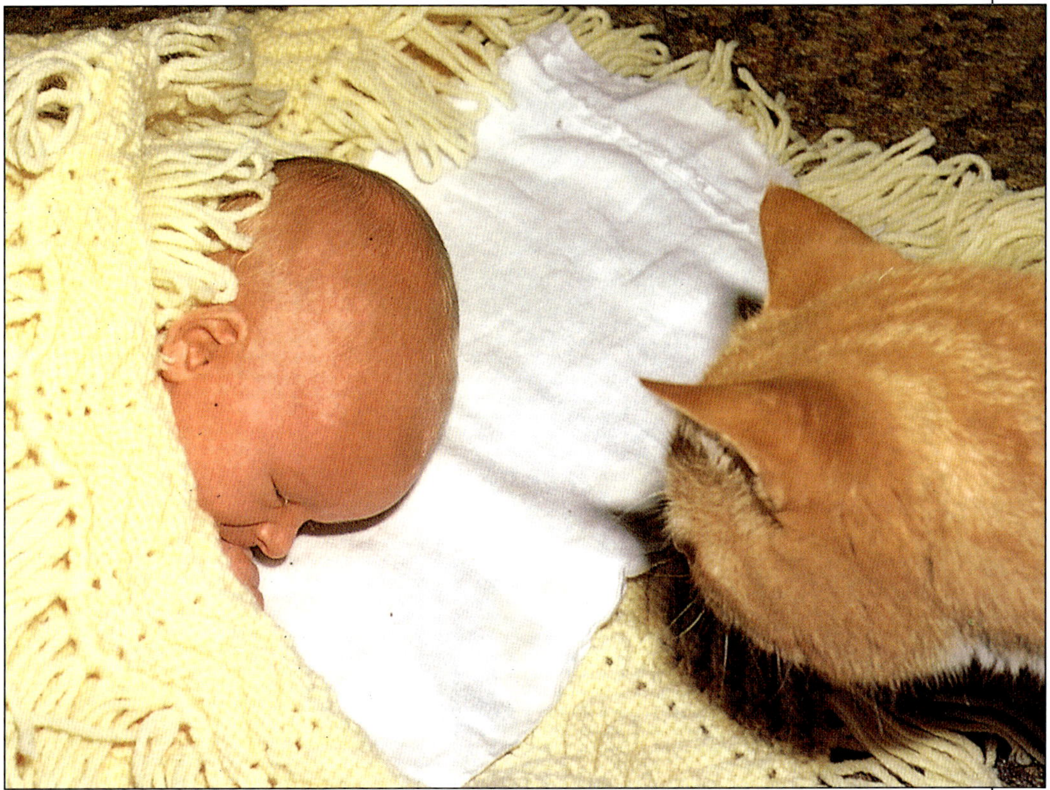

**BELOW** *Quiet, peaceful activities are more likely to attract the interest and participation of cats, although their attention spans can be pretty short. Natural circumstances normally involve a wild cat in any given activity for relatively brief periods.*

the first couple of encounters, however, felines and young humans can learn to enjoy each other's company.

The relationship of your cat with children should begin before the first physical contact is made. Because children are slightly easier to train – only by a whisker – direct your instructions to the child.

He should wait for the cat to approach him, which really won't take that long given the curious nature of most cats. When the approach does come, he should not reach out to grab or pet the cat. Instead he should slowly and smoothly hold out his hand towards the cat's nose, for some getting-to-know-you sniffing. If that seems to bring an overall friendly reaction from the cat, the child can pet her gently and talk to her softly. Having the child use the cat's name, or other "cuddle" words that the cat seems to appreciate at other times, will increase the chances of the encounter being a promising one.

Regardless of how well a cat-child session may seem to be proceeding, babies and young children should *never* be left alone with a cat. No matter how much you trust the cat, or the child, there is always the possibility of one of them overreacting to something the other does and attempting to inflict pain on the other. What started out as a happy relationship can turn into an ugly one when you have to decide who did what to whom and whether the cat is stable enough to stay in the family (it's never a question of whether or not to get rid of the kid). The cats are usually the losers in these cases, which is unfortunate because the real blame should be placed on the parents who failed to follow this most basic rule of cat-child relationships.

Cats that have been introduced to children in a casual, non-confrontational manner are generally very open to meetings with other children. If the child can be contained within the cat's acceptable parameters for human behaviour towards her, the relationship can proceed much like any cat-human bond, complete with heartfelt affection.

## BONDING WITH YOUR CAT

Many of us mistakenly treat our pets as children. Because of their drive for comfort and security in their lives, they will be happy to accommodate us as far as it serves their needs. However, to expect a cat to give as much as it gets is a certain route to disappointment, as it also is to believe subconsciously that the cat will always be there for you, even though you know she probably cannot live more than 10 to 15 years.

You should give as much as you can to the relationship and allow your cat the freedom to do the same. Even human-to-human relationships where a tally is kept of all that is given and taken by each party are headed for problems. Expecting equality of give and take will not lead to the sort of bonding that will give you and your cat the most enjoyable relationship.

In animal terms, bonding is the pairing of two creatures who develop a long-term connection as the result of shared experiences and dependency.

Bonding is not only satisfying, it is also essential in maintaining a well-mannered cat as part of your life and home.

The process begins from your very first contact with the cat, whether that occurs when she is just a kitten or when she is well into maturity. Usually you have no idea of what the cat experienced before she came into your life. She may have socialized with other cats and humans, she may have had no contact with others or she may have suffered plenty of negative contact.

You must first communicate to her that she is safe with and accepted by you. Long before you begin to think about showing her around the house or beginning her training, you must establish the maximum comfort and security level possible. Only then will she be receptive.

When you first bring the cat into your home, don't overwhelm her by allowing the family to crowd around and try to touch her. It's best to introduce her to this new environment on a one-to-one basis. Gently allow her to look around and examine whatever she will at first. When she seems somewhat familiarized, bring in members of the family individually and let them gently touch her and get to know her, and her them. Other pets, which should have been kept in another room until now, should be introduced last, although not after too long a wait.

She won't have any understanding of your words at this point, but she will be on constant watch for any clues that she can draw from your tone and touch. Gently and soothingly are how both should be delivered.

At first, and probably for a longer period than you're going to appreciate, you won't get much tenderness from your cat. She has an entirely new territory to establish. After all, who knows what dangers may lurk in it? Give her the "space" she needs to discover just how completely safe and secure you've made her.

She may not want much physical contact at all at first, but you can rely on her intelligence to keep her posted on just who it is that seems to be fulfilling her every need. Eventually, if she hasn't been pressed too hard on the issue, she will probably initiate contact on her own. That's your cue to really lay on the love and affection in as large a quantity as you can manage while still maintaining that atmosphere of calmness and gentleness.

Of course, if the cat has not taken it on herself to do this within a week or so of being brought into the home, you may need to coax it out of her. Approach slowly, as near to her level as you can – sitting, if that's the best you can do; kneeling is better yet; hands and knees is still better; and on your belly is best of all. Speak gently and soothingly. Some morsels of food would definitely not hurt.

Once the bonding has begun and has then continued on a regular basis, it might become a ritual that the cat now expects as part of its everyday life.

**OPPOSITE** *By providing ample quantities of all the basics of a cat's life we have made room for a much more social existence than wild felines normally enjoy. We've eliminated most of the environmental reasons for competition.*

**LEFT** *Any spot that provides the comfort and security that they constantly crave will be attractive to our cats. For a deeper relationship try to become part of that comfort and security by observing what it is that gives these qualities to your cat and how you can enhance them.*

Cats do not respond in the same way to training. Our approach must be entirely different from that we take in training other animals.

Dogs strive to learn your commands for little more than the security of having pleased their master – or, more correctly from the dog's perspective, the leader of their pack. Cats' motives are a bit more inner-directed (some might say downright self-centred).

The positive motivators in a cat's life are food, comfort (most often translated as warmth) and play/company. Negative motivators to a cat are wetness, discomfort (most often translated as anything but warmth) and loud noises.

## PUNISHMENT AND REWARD

You'll notice that physical punishment, restraint or force does not find a place on either of our lists. This is because the reaction of most cats to such direct, purposeful contact is simple avoidance. "If you want to be that rough," the cat is telling you as it slinks quickly from the room, "I'll see you later." Perhaps the cat will respond in kind with claws and teeth to the first few physical efforts at discipline, but even this will soon be abandoned for retreat. Too many such encounters can leave a psychological imprint in the cat's mind against the "offending" human that can be nearly impossible to mend.

Even sharp verbal commands can have this effect. While a quick "No!" or "Stop!" will probably stop the cat from scratching at the furniture leg, too many of these will leave you with a nervous, retiring and shy animal.

When you yell at your cat, you are making a mental connection between your harsh command and whatever it is that you don't want the cat to be doing. But the cat forgets what it was doing immediately on hearing your sharp tone and instead identifies the discomfort with its source – you. For some reason which the animal cannot fathom, you are causing it discomfort.

This is the reason that so many animal behaviourists today recommend indirect deterrents to stop unwanted behaviour. A ball of paper or a short, gentle squirt from a water pistol have power equal to a harsh command in stopping the cat doing wrong, but the animal generally won't trace the source of its discomfort back to you. Consequently, you'll be able to repeat the deterrent as many times as necessary until the cat learns to cease the offending activity without your being identified as the bad guy.

A word of caution: even balls of paper and squirts of water can be carried too far, from the cat's perspective. In a sense, they are being delivered by some unseen enemy and constant, unexpected "attacks" can lead to a very nervous cat. Moderation is crucial. Take corrective measures only when absolutely necessary.

On the other hand, use the positive reinforcements as much as possible. Nothing perks up a

**RIGHT** *Patience, persistence and repetition are the prerequisites for developing any new forms of behaviour, or tricks, in your cat. As under wild conditions, the cat must come to recognize the benefits that the new behaviour holds for it.*

**OPPOSITE** *Food is one of the strongest motivators for our cats. Special treats can bring them to heights of performance.*

cat's attention span and memory capacity like a morsel of its favourite food, even more so if it's something that's not available every day.

For example, to teach the cat her name, hold a bit of the food out towards her and call her by name. If she comes, give her the food, speak in low, soothing tones of praise and pet or stroke her in whatever manner she most likes. Repeat this only a few times at a sitting to avoid losing the cat's attention and your patience, but try to do it at least once a day for a couple of weeks.

Many cat owners have followed this process using food at mealtime instead of the snack morsel. Each time they dished out the cat's meal, they

**LEFT** *Cats will develop their own special behaviour and tricks to achieve their own ends. These actions seem to develop more quickly when food is involved.*

**OPPOSITE** *This may be all the response that a "come" command draws from your cat, not because it doesn't understand the command but because it isn't choosing to obey just now.*

called her name and made a fuss of her when she came. At mealtime it's important that the training and praise do not interfere with the cat's eating or the opposite effect from that intended might be achieved.

Whatever training you choose to attempt with your cat and whatever successes you achieve, don't fool yourself that you've taught the cat the concepts of right and wrong. These are human words, without any true meaning for any other living creatures on earth.

Cats never feel remorse for any of their actions. They never feel accomplished because of what they have learned and performed. What they feel is their own current level of comfort and security. "Yeah, sure, I learned to do a triple somersault from the top of the shelves, catching my catnip mouse on the way down," they might say, if they could talk. "But how about dinner? Isn't it about that time?"

They will begin doing something and continue to do it only as long as they realize a direct benefit through the action. Conversely, they will cease doing something and not do it again only as long as they realize a negative effect on themselves because of it.

Nevertheless, training your cat is a worthwhile pursuit, requiring extreme patience and understanding on your part. You must be willing to go back to the drawing board time and time again. But it will add a great deal to both your lives. The benefits that you might draw from a well-trained cat are obvious, but cats too gain from the training. They are highly inquisitive animals that will thrive on the stimulation that your efforts will provide for their minds. After all, sleeping for 18 hours per day doesn't provide much in the way of mind-bending challenges.

## LAYING DOWN RULES OF BEHAVIOUR

Like his comic namesake, Garfield was a terror. Whether the effort to bring his behaviour into check had never been mounted or had simply been given up as of no use we never really knew. By the time we came across him, his furniture

shredding, drapery tearing and antagonistic attitude towards all visitors was pretty much taken for granted. His humans shared his home, and even provided his food and water, but otherwise he lived mostly independently of them.

To their credit, we never heard Garfield's humans mention getting rid of him as a solution to their mounting problem. It probably never even occurred to them. They are basically gentle souls, who honestly believe that animals have rights equal to humans and live their lives according to such principles.

On the other hand, they had done something of a disservice to Garfield by never enforcing any sense of what was acceptable and what was not. For the lack of a few strong words and perhaps a squirt or two of water in the early development of their cat-human relationship, they had allowed the black Persian to grow into a cat that few people wanted to be around.

Cats need to be shown what is and what is not acceptable behaviour. Don't think for a moment that cats in the wild are not taught these valuable lessons by their mother, other cats and other animals. Survival depends upon the passing on and enforcement of certain "rules" from one generation to the next.

But when the cat is in a man-made environment, the situation changes in two very important ways. First, there are additional aspects that need to be incorporated into her behaviour so that she is an acceptable member of the household. Second, while nature generally relies much more heavily on negative teaching aids, the human teacher will be more successful when using positive reinforcement.

One negative enforcement that you will want to use is a loud, harsh "No!" Consistency in the use of this command whenever the cat is committing the unwanted behaviour is essential, although too much use of the word can lead to a nervous cat. Most cats will get the idea long before you've shouted too often.

Punishment must always come while the cat is engaged in the activity you want to curb. Telling the cat "no" after she has left the scene of the

**ABOVE** *Punishment of your cat should never include striking with the hand, or even the threat of striking. This can only cause the cat to view hands as a source of pain and discomfort.*

**OPPOSITE** *As cute and cuddly as any kitten may look, you're setting up your relationship with the cat for failure if you expect that there won't be some trying moments.*

**LEFT** *A typical cat response to chastisement is simply to hide from its source, unlike a dog which would attempt to seek forgiveness for whatever it had done wrong.*

scratched furniture and is eating from her bowl, even if you first carry her back to the furniture, sends some confusing signals. The scratching is in the past. It's already gone from the cat's mind. Why are you shouting at her for eating?

Beyond all forms of punishment, positive reinforcement will bring a cat over to your way of thinking much faster. Feline motivations are these: comfort, security, food and water. Pleasing you with her performance appears nowhere on that list, except as far as it is a means to accomplish one of these.

The first three are the most useful in trying to train a cat. A morsel of some favourite snack is

always welcome but gentle, soothing words and soft stroking are equally effective, because of their direct relationship in the mind of the cat to its comfort and security.

Your praise for everything the cat does correctly, even the smallest things, should be extreme and exaggerated. Punishment for those actions that you consider undesirable should move in the other direction. It should be reserved and restrained. You might even overlook some of the small problems.

Every breed of domestic cat and nearly every species of wild cat has been trained with these principles. Of course, different individuals have different capacities: some adapt much better to training than others.

When a new problem (or one that was previously corrected) surfaces in your cat, look for the underlying causes before you begin any corrective measures. Perhaps the inadvertent removal of the scratching post during housecleaning is the real reason for the recent attacks on the furniture. Replace the scratching post and the chances are good that the furniture-scratching will cease. Maybe you're not cleaning the litter box regularly enough and that's the cat's justification for turning elsewhere. Perhaps your cat is experiencing some new emotional stress or physical illness.

## GRUDGES AND RESENTMENTS

Kaybee is fat by anyone's stretch of the imagination. Her belly drags on the floor when she walks to such a degree that she actually rubs fur from her underside. Her legs are bowed. Picking her up is no easy chore.

But in her mind, she's simply well-fed and maintained in the comfort to which she has become accustomed. Is it any wonder that she resents the efforts of our friend Pauline to enforce a bit of dieting?

That's right, she resents her reduced rations. Resents, as human as that emotion might sound, is the only word that's appropriate here. Kaybee has exchanged her previous greetings at the front door each evening with as purposeful a walk as she can manage in the opposite direction when Pauline gets home from work. She no longer "talks" to her in those little chats the two of them used to share.

As we write this, the diet's been under way for only a few weeks, so there's no way of knowing how far Kaybee will continue her grudge. She may very well come up with new ways to send her message to Pauline. Just as likely, she may call a halt to her protest over time.

Cats definitely hold grudges and feel resentment, although generally for much more basic and understandable reasons than we humans. Whenever they perceive a deprivation of some of the basic necessities that they've come to expect us to provide, they will register their complaints. They're just not as happy and contented as they were before, and it shows in their behaviour. That can mean anything from a simple lessening of enthusiasm to acts that might best be described as spiteful.

However, what at first appears to be an act of spite by a cat is more often than not motivated by anxiety or boredom. This is probably the underlying cause of Felix attacking the leg of the couch while you're out, even though he is normally happy to use the scratching post in the kitchen. He has no way of knowing how soon you intend

**OPPOSITE** *Rarely will cats be caught in the act of doing something that their owner has made clear is undesirable. This doesn't mean they won't continue the activity. They just won't get caught.*

**RIGHT** *Seeking the comfort and security that are the prime motivations in her life, your cat may try to avoid contact with you when she sees you as a disrupting force.*

to return. Maybe over the previous seven days you've been out for the same amount of time and Felix hasn't reacted to it. But, for whatever cat reason he may have, today he needed you close. When you weren't there his comfort and security levels dropped and anxiety built up within him, eventually finding this outlet.

## WHO, ME?

You've probably noticed that whenever any indiscretions take place, catching the guilty party in the act (or even in the appearance of guilt) is just about impossible. For example, consider the shelf filled with favourite and fragile collectables that has also attracted the attentions of a cat for whatever reason – perhaps warm air collects there, perhaps there's a special feeling of security, perhaps there is some other reason that you can't fathom. You've made it clear to the cat that the shelf is off-limits, and you never see the cat on it. However, as you approach that room you hear the "thud, thud" of a cat making its way down to the floor from some elevated position. As you enter the room, you see the cat seated on the floor, well away from the shelf, grooming. Sleepily he looks up at you, as if to say, "Oh, hello there. Fancy meeting you. I've just been sitting here on the floor for the past hour or so, grooming myself."

At times like these it's easy to believe in the concept of cat lies. Anyone who has spent much time at all around cats has at least one or two tales that seem to prove beyond a shadow of a doubt that cats do in fact tell lies, and quite often.

**RIGHT** *An action such as this that gives the cat a measure of reward can become difficult to curb if you don't react immediately and consistently.*

**ABOVE** *Our houseplants are a particular source of interest to our cats. They have a natural attraction to plants, and will claw and chew them.*

However, lying may be too human a concept for what the cats really are doing. You'll recall that comfort and security are among the chief motivators in the life of the cat. What better way for the animal to maintain some control over these areas than with secrecy about what it's been up to and where it's been doing it. The cat's philosophy here is this: "Nobody saw me, I didn't do it." The portrayal of innocence on your entry into the room may seem like plain dishonesty, but is, in fact another natural mechanism to avoid loss of comfort and security. If you didn't see the cat doing the forbidden action, there won't be any yelling or other punishments.

One of the most widespread bits of misinformation about domestic cats is the myth of the finicky cat. While individual cats most certainly do possess and regularly demonstrate their preferences for one type of food over another, much of this picky behaviour – probably much more than can ever be proved conclusively – relates to the quality of the food rather than the type. By quality we're referring to the taste and smell of the food when it's served rather than the original ingredients that went into it.

Exactly how strong and how important the cat's sense of smell really is has not yet been determined with any certainty. It is safe, however, to place it somewhere well above our own but still below that of the dog. In its simplest terms, this means cats can smell a great many more things about their food than we can.

Of course, it goes almost without saying that spoiled or spoiling food will curtail even the heartiest of appetites, but this question of quality cuts much deeper than that. Maybe the chemical of the plastic bowl is slowly leaching its way into the atmosphere, releasing some pretty strong and repulsive odours, at least to the more sensitive nostrils of the cat. Perhaps the smell of the chemical cleansers used to wash the bowl still linger, under the magnified inspection of a cat's nose. Or maybe the bowl hasn't been cleansed sufficiently to remove the rotting smell of a meal that the cat already turned down a couple of days earlier in the week.

Although this is not a book about cat health and diet, it seems appropriate to add a cautionary note at this point: *cats are carnivores; they need meat to survive in health.* The animal rights anti-meat lobby has tried to convince us that our pets can get by just fine on a totally vegetarian diet. This may be true for dogs (although we're never going to eliminate the excitement that they feel over a piece of meat) but it most definitely is not true for cats. A diet completely lacking in any meat is

**LEFT** *A secluded, out-of-the-way spot for dining is a great comfort to your cat, allowing for relaxed and unhurried eating.*

**LEFT** *Even well-cleaned food bowls can carry lingering odours undetectable by humans that can deter cats from eating. Cleaning chemicals can also leave distasteful odours.*

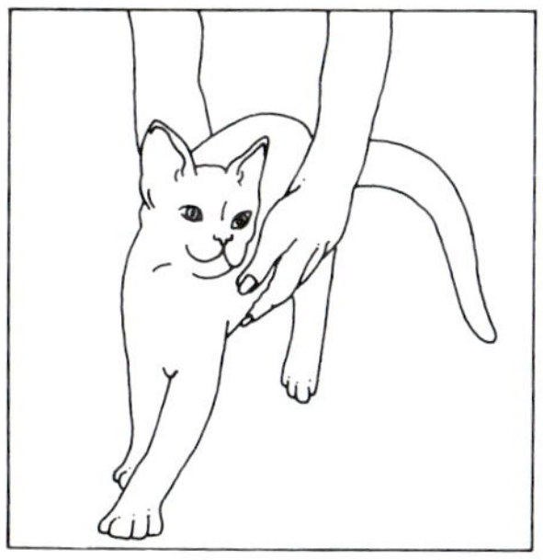

## The Rib Test

The rib test remains a reasonably effective guide to whether or not a cat's weight is correct. If you cannot feel each rib individually, without exerting undue pressure, then the cat is probably too fat. If the ridges of the cat's ribs feel like pencils, the chances are that it is not being fed enough, or that it is suffering from a condition which needs immediate attention from your vet.

more than likely depriving the cat of some nutrients that are only available from animal flesh, such as the arachidonic fatty acids and ready-to-use vitamin A.

Another contributing factor to the feeding problems of a cat that has been termed a finicky eater may be environmental. Feeding is a time when an animal's guard is temporarily let down. Therefore, eating is most comfortably enjoyed in quiet, seclusion and security. Feeding bowls placed in high traffic areas of the home obviously do not meet these criteria.

### THE FAT CAT

Obesity is a very real problem in our cats – indeed, it's a problem for nearly all species of animal that are kept as domestic pets. We humans in the developed world have shared this failing with our companion animals!

A true definition of an overweight cat is hard to come by. We've discussed this subject with several different veterinarians and heard nearly as many different opinions. Society's view of feline obesity seems to be in a constant state of change. Also, some breeds carry their weight less obviously than others. Although some experts would go further with their definitions, your cat is probably fat if you can't feel her ribs without applying more pressure than you do when stroking her.

Sometimes excess weight can be attributed to a cat's physiology, but more often it is the result of a personality quirk – there are some cats that will eat to excess whenever they get the chance.

Of course, even these cats need human assistance to eat their way to an overweight state. Food left in the bowl all day encourages the cat to eat just as an open box of chocolates sitting on the end table while we watch television tempts us. No cat needs food to be available throughout the day. Two meals should be provided, and no more.

If you're already feeding at the proper rate, perhaps you should consider a switch to a higher quality food. Advertising claims to the contrary, some commercially available foods are packed with fillers and starches that are of little use to the cat's body, except when it comes to putting on

**OPPOSITE** *Restricted diet, higher-quality food and increased exercise can all be part of the solution to the problem of the overweight cat. How much of each one is necessary varies from one situation to the next.*

**BELOW** *Preventing behaviour that some people find offensive can often be simple. In this case, shutting the toilet lid and providing an alternative water source would probably solve the problem.*

excess weight. In the past few years some new brands have emerged that provide the ultimate balanced diet. These are generally not available on grocers' shelves, but a trip to the pet shop is worth while for the potential weight-loss in your cat.

Another reason for a fat cat is lack of sufficient daily exercise. Cats are natural-born slackers when it comes to physical exertion, and they certainly don't worry about their waistlines. They need some additional incentive to get moving.

You can provide that added motivation. You probably know your cat's favourite form of play. Engage him in games for as long as his interest holds. You can also up the frequency of your play periods. If you play with him for 15 minutes every other day or so, change to 15 minutes every day. If you already play for 15 minutes every day, perhaps you could find another quarter-hour elsewhere in the day for a separate session.

## Scavenging

It has been said by certain theorists that to a cat no meal is really worth the eating unless it has involved the eater in at least some token effort to beg, steal or hunt. Certainly, even the fattest of domestic cats will go to considerable trouble to steal, even if it is merely knocking down and ripping open a box of its own dried catfood to win the unambitious reward of a few illicit morsels.

**ABOVE** *Cats find many ways of telling us what they want us to do and what they don't want us to do. Such as, "Do you really have to leave on this business trip?"*

Most of us have heard of the elephants' graveyard, that mythical place where all elephants go to die. The legend could just as easily have been developed about a cats' graveyard. There would be as much truth to the latter notion as the former.

Such mass graveyards, filled with the bones of hundreds of thousands of one species, do not actually exist, except in the form of human cemeteries. However, it's easy to understand how such a myth arose.

The animal response to pain and illness is different to the human one. Animals' first instinct is not to seek out help, comfort and relief from others of their kind, or from human housemates in the case of our cats. They don't have our scientific understanding of what's really amiss under these circumstances. Instead, they are left to their own analysis of the situation. And what they perceive the pain or discomfort to be is the result of a sudden attack by some enemy, invisible though that enemy might be.

In the face of such an attack, the reasonable animal behaviour is to escape and hide. The most secure hiding place in the cat's territory is generally selected as a refuge.

Cats that are allowed to roam freely outdoors and are familiar with a much larger territory often just seem to vanish, never to return. Rather than running away, as is commonly assumed, many of these cats have simply curled up and died in some vacant building or stack of rubbish.

During episodes of illness, compassion from a human is rather meaningless while the pain or discomfort goes right on attacking. The one

exception may be the cat that has been conditioned to view a human's lap or arms as packed with security and comfort.

The sudden absence of a cat from its normal "rounds" about the house may therefore be among the very first symptoms of injury or illness. As we've explained elsewhere in this book, there can be other reasons for a reclusive cat, but if the change in routine comes on suddenly a trip to the vet may be in order.

## SOURCES OF STRESS

Injury and illness are just two of the many things that we take for granted in our everyday lives which pose great mysteries to our cats.

**ABOVE** *Cats also do not understand our attempts to heal them. Splints and bandages such as those on this kitten's leg are seen as something restrictive and often as an invasion of their body.*

Other aspects of this strange human world will continue to baffle the cat throughout its life. The sudden change in attitude towards the cat's use of furniture when a new living-room suite is brought into the house is beyond Kitty's comprehension. It's not that difficult to understand her reaction of avoiding the living room and possibly her humans, who seem to have gone insane and are suddenly scolding for activities that yesterday were perfectly acceptable. The new furniture represents nothing more than the loss of much beloved, familiar territory to Kitty. She just doesn't have the capacity to understand or share your excitement about this acquisition.

Similar reactions can arise to nearly anything new that we bring into the cat's territory, which coincidentally is also our home. New babies, new pets, rearranged furniture all represent change, and often change accompanied by new attitudes on our part. Moving to a new house is probably the change with maximum impact on the cat, who sees only the loss of familiar territory and a massive need for readjustment.

Another source of cat stress is being forced to spend excessive time alone. This is not widely recognized because of the independent nature of our cats in comparison to other companion animals. It's true that cats are not pack animals but they do need social contact, with other cats where possible or with their human housemates as a substitute.

Any absence longer than a normal workday, if repeated regularly, is probably enough to cause some degree of loneliness in most cats. Those cat owners who find themselves out of the house for such extended periods may want to bring a second cat into the home, being careful that the two felines are compatible with one another.

Many aspects of the man-made world into which we bring our cats can cause them stress, although the amount of stress and the reaction to it will vary from one cat to the next. Just like humans, cats vary in their capacity to deal with stressful situations. And, just as in humans, stress can lead to illness in our cats.

Early symptoms of stress can include drastic changes in normal daily activity, increased amounts of time spent in self-grooming, loss of or increase in appetite, change in the condition of the coat and dullness in the eyes. These, of course, are the early symptoms for a great many cat ailments, so home diagnosis is not practical. If a few such symptoms show up and cannot be explained through your observations on your cat, a visit to the veterinarian is in order.

Many of these same symptoms will be noticed in a depressed cat. Don't get us wrong – we're not advocates of the pet psychologist trade that caters to the animals of the rich and trendy. But we are convinced that animals, especially sensitive ones like our cats, do feel a sense of loss when

**RIGHT** *The loss of some member of the household, whether through death or simply because they moved away from home, can send some cats into depression.*

someone leaves their lives and they do experience a form of depression over that loss. In other words, cats mourn.

They also have many more occasions to mourn than humans do. We've never seen any evidence to point to the fact that cats understand the concept of death, but loss is another thing entirely. The cat feels loss whenever someone from its familiar world is no longer there. This interferes with its feelings of comfort and security, and the cat is therefore anxious about the change.

Death of a family member – and this description includes other pets that share the home – is one reason for loss, but to the cat it is the same when

**LEFT** *Sometimes the addition of a new family member can snap a mourning cat out of its depression over the loss of a previous member.*

a teenager goes off to college or when the family is broken by divorce. Even something as temporary as a member of the family away for vacation or on an extended business trip has been known to trigger this mourning response in some cats. The fact that the missing individual will be resurfacing from time to time just isn't in the cat's frame of reference.

Kitty's first reaction will be several thorough searches of the home for the missing individual over the first few days of separation. Often, these investigations are accompanied with a regular series of questioning meows.

The next step will usually be a period of sulky, sluggish behaviour. The cat will have lost just about all of her normal appetite for play, quite possibly for food as well. She'll spend much more time than normal just lying about, not in sleep but in apparent boredom.

At this point, intervention is suggested to prevent the more severe symptoms. Perhaps the cat's focus on the lost companion can be broken with the introduction of a new member to the family. If your conditions permit, this is often an excellent time to introduce a second cat to the home. Having more people over to the house can also help to fill the void.

Also, you might try to "jump-start" Kitty out of her malaise. Add some variety to her life by introducing some new games, particularly exciting games of the ambush variety. Try some new toys, and follow the guidelines in the next chapter to make those toys all the more appealing to her. Think up something new to add to her dinner menu. Allow her a few extra sessions with the catnip

Do anything you can think of to divert the cat's attention from the loss she is feeling. Make certain that all other things that relate to her levels of comfort and security are maintained, and, if possible, enhanced.

Animals have relatively short attention spans, so you should be able to fill her life so full that she can't help but snap out of it before too long.

Adult visitors to Gramma's home would smile in disbelief at stories of the rambunctious antics of Quincy – at least those who visited without children in tow. There was simply no way that they could accept such tales about the pleasingly plump calico. The only Quincy they had ever seen was a placid, retiring cat that did little beyond lie on Gramma's lap and stretch and yawn occasionally. To them that was the only personality that Quincy exhibited. Even the basketful of cat toys, from rubber milk bottles to catnip-filled cloth mice, that Gramma had collected for him never seemed to attract more than a passing glance.

But in the presence of children a completely different cat emerged. A roughhousing, fleet-footed, even lovingly aggressive fool of a cat occupied Quincy's mind and body whenever young playmates were available. Every conceivable game seemed to come immediately to mind, from ankle-attack tag to all-out wrestling, the rougher the better.

The one trait that Quincy seemed able to carry into either of his personalities was that of gentleness. No matter how rough the play might become, Quincy never used his claws or teeth.

While such a completely split personality is not at all common in cats – at least not when it comes to play – much else among the attitudes that Quincy exhibited can be generalized across domestic cats as a whole.

Cats love to play. They even show much originality in the play they invent, such as stalking a spot of light on the wall, and in attracting us to take part with them. But they also have some pretty strong rules about their play.

**LEFT** *One of the most important criteria in play for cats is near-constant motion. Expensive toys are not necessary to provide this.*

All but the most malfunctioning kittens need play. It's the primary means of learning the early lessons about how to survive as a cat. Even kittens of wild cats, from the bobcat to the African lion, spend much of their early weeks in play. Those kittens that are too weak or sick or otherwise unable to engage in the full extent of play with their siblings will have a much tougher time of it throughout their lives.

Most cats carry some of the playful instinct with them into adulthood. They even continue to need the activity, particularly those that are cooped up all day by themselves in small apartments or even large houses. For these "home alone" cats, the play period that follows the arrival of the humans in the late afternoon and evening is a special time. The activity contributes not only some vital exercise, but also an opportunity for bonding and growing closer. Even rough-house play, if your cat has demonstrated a liking for it, will serve this purpose.

Laid out like this in print, such set-aside play-time may sound like an overly taxing drain on your crucial time after a hectic day at the office, but just 10 or 15 minutes is a long time for your cat. Wouldn't such a brief respite be a pleasant way for you to wind down as well?

## PROVIDING PLAY

Movement is the critical aspect in cat play. If it's moving, the cat's interested. This explains why the hundreds of dollars'-worth of toys scattered about the house just don't seem to provide an adequate substitute for your hand or foot. Those toys do nothing on their own. They just lie there. You're the energy behind any of the interesting motions they manage.

Think like a mouse. The little rodent scurries as fast as it can from one bit of cover to the next, stopping at each to peer out nervously before starting again on its fleeting way. This is the type of movement that cats most enjoy.

They also enjoy the pounce and capture, which is the ultimate goal of any hunt (now replaced with play). If the cat manages to catch and chew on the mouse (toy) every so often during the play period, his interest will be maintained for considerably longer.

In the wild state, much of the play behaviour of a cat will disappear with maturity. The regular pursuit of enough prey to survive and continue the species brings a much more serious aspect to the whole affair, not to mention the constant attention to avoiding dangerous enemies.

However, in your house most of these worries have been eliminated, which influences your cat's continued interest in play for two reasons. First, by providing nearly all of the cat's food, you are assuming the role of a parent cat and allowing your feline to retain much of its kitten-ness into and through adulthood. Secondly, it is as well to accept that the hunting instinct never dies and that the well-adjusted cat must find some new routes into which it can channel all the energy that would normally be directed in this manner. Active play is the perfect substitute.

**OPPOSITE** *New places to explore, regardless of how simple and commonplace, are like amusement park rides to our cats. Don't miss the opportunity to give a box or bag to your cat.*

**RIGHT** *Some play is more welcome than others, as this kitten may learn soon after dropping on the sleeping adult.*

There are some common cat games that will interest almost any feline. The clichéd activities such as batting at a suspended ball of yarn have become clichéd because so many million cats have perpetuated them down through the generations. Hide and seek, with either you or your Quincy hiding and then ambushing the other as he walks by, is also a standard.

Every cat and owner will also invent their own special play. Remain open to each new opportunity that presents itself during play period and you'll find yourself and your cat doing just that. It's likely that whatever little games the cat comes up with will be clues to what it enjoys most.

Blanket chase, where the owner's hand is attacked while moving beneath a blanket, rug, towel or some similarly soft covering, will entice even sedentary felines. Hide the toy, in which some of the cat's favourite possessions are hidden about the house, will play upon the natural feline curiosity. This is a particularly good game for you to set up for the cat before leaving for work each morning.

These are some of the games that have proven most enjoyable with the majority of cats we've owned or known, but they are only a starting point and not an all-inclusive list. The important aspect of cat play is not form but motion.

Euphrates is a blue bi-colour Sphynx, who, to the best of our knowledge, has never experienced the outdoors except when transported in her kennel from one indoor location to the next. This is probably the way it should be. The Sphynx is a man-made breed, refined since 1966 for its hairless quality. Even the slightest draught on an otherwise warm summer's day can send these cats into spasms of shivers.

To owners of many other breeds and the ever-hardy moggies this may sound cruel indeed. But Euphrates, and other cats like her, probably has

**ABOVE** *Cats that have experienced the outdoors generally have a longing to return there again and again, if only for very brief periods at a time.*

**LEFT** *Some cats genuinely have no desire ever to leave the comfort and security of their homes. The attraction of new sights and sounds just doesn't pull as strongly on them.*

never even thought of the possibility of some world beyond the one she shares with her humans.

The outdoor world would be a terrifying, hostile place, filled with things she didn't understand and had never encountered before. Her personality really could not cope with it all. And, if temperatures dipped from those of a very warm day, she would have a hard time dealing with it physically, as well.

She doesn't know she's missing anything and, given her delicate nature, quite probably she isn't. Cats that have never experienced life in the outdoors generally don't feel any need for it. They've built their entire lives around the world that they find within the safe and secure walls of their home.

On the other hand, a cat who has got the feel of the outdoors will probably always have some need for an occasional return there. Like all living things, cats who aren't restricted by some special circumstances generally do enjoy a change of scenery and some fresh air. It's still a new concept – one that is often met with ridicule and disagreement – that cats can be taken for a walk like dogs.

The big difference is that cats are more prone to resist the mechanisms involved in taking that walk than their canine counterparts. As with everything you want to teach to your cat, remember that he is motivated mostly by his own needs and wants rather than what you want for him. Unlike a dog, he's not going to submit readily to collar and leash simply because it will make you happy.

He needs to see the direct benefits early in the process to warm up to the idea of having any form of restraint placed on him. Here is where a Catch 22 situation takes shape. You shouldn't really allow your cat outdoors without that restraint, but he's going to resist that restraint until he's seen the wonders of the outdoors.

Many members of the cat fancy solve this problem by never addressing it. They simply allow the cat outdoors alone or under constant observation. This is unfair to many cats who are not equipped to deal with all the dangers of the outdoors, both natural and man-made. Even the most carefully watched cat will easily escape from his intended area of roaming if he wants. Commands to come back will likely fall on deaf ears.

That said, clearly some cats will adapt far better to the great outdoors than others, and their territorial environment will itself vary greatly: from urban sprawl to rural farmland. Use discretion, therefore, but bear in mind that nearly all cats can

**OPPOSITE** *A harness does not have the threatening feel about the neck that a collar can impart.*

**RIGHT** *Contrary to popular misbelief, cats can be taught to walk at the end of a leash. Some come to enjoy the experience.*

be taught to walk on a leash, given enough time and patience on the part of the teacher.

## LEARNING TO WALK ON THE LEASH

As a first step, a soft but sturdy harness needs to be chosen. (A harness is better than a collar because it is less threatening to the cat psyche than a stranglehold.) The cat's natural curiosity is your biggest ally at this point. Toss the harness on the floor, near (not in) the cat's bed, and leave it there for several days. This will give the cat a chance to examine the harness on its own terms and to accept it as just another piece of the house.

When he seems to be comfortable with the harness and is no longer purposefully walking around it, try slipping it over his head during a play period. Continue to talk to the cat in a normal voice. If he accepts the harness, heap his favourite praise on him. Remove the harness gently, again with praise, after just a few minutes.

**OPPOSITE** *The outdoors offers additional exercise that can bring variety to the cat's life while helping him to stay fit.*

**LEFT** *Being trained to the leash allows your cat to go safely into fairly built-up areas under your control.*

If he rejects it, go back to playing for another few minutes, then try it again. If he rejects it again, forget it for that day. Never force him to submit to the harness. Try again the next day, adding a few morsels of his favourite snack as you are placing the harness over his head.

Repeat the process again the next day, leaving the harness over his head for several minutes longer. Next day try a longer period and so on, for a week or more.

Next try the process with the addition of fastening the under-belly strap of the harness. Many cats, by this time, won't be put off by the additional restraint but if yours is annoyed by the concept, remove the harness immediately and gently. Try again the next day.

After several days of wearing the full harness, the cat should be ready for the leash. Snap it to the harness, pick up your end and allow the cat to lead wherever he wants. You don't want to give the impression that you are somehow threatening the cat, or you'll be using the leash to extract him from under the nearest piece of furniture. Just let the cat lead, but also let him know that you and he are now connected by the leash.

After about a week of doing this for longer periods each day, add the following stage at what would normally be the end of your session. Step a few feet in front of the cat, kneel or lie at his level, hold out a morsel of his favourite treat, give your "come" command and very slightly tug on the leash – don't pull the cat. In another week you'll be ready to forget the morsel of food and reward the cat with praise alone. Increase the distance until you've persuaded the cat into something resembling an actual walk on the leash.

You and your cat are now more than a month from the beginning of this training period. Now you can attempt your first actual outing. The garden is the most non-threatening location for this and the next few trials. Finally, when the two of you are strolling about the yard, comfortable with each other's role in this strange affair, try walking in a nearby park.

Few of the neighbourhood cats even tried to challenge Tiger on his "turf" any longer. For that matter, few creatures of any sort in the neighbourhood were foolhardy enough to encroach on the acre or so of ground, trees, garden, driveway, garage and house that he claimed as his territory.

The dog and human family with whom Tiger shared his home were permitted to roam freely throughout the site, but even they tended to respect the scarred feline scrapper and give him quarter more often than not.

So Tiger lived for the occasional wandering stray from outside the neighbourhood. He relished every such opportunity to add to his legend, which over the years included wins beyond those of even the most able prize-fighters. Other male cats accounted for the majority of his "notches", but many a day – and an occasional raccoon or opossum – retreated before his ferocity. Without knowing it, we often reinforced Tiger's dominance over the site by breaking up a fight and chasing the intruding cat.

At about the age of five, in the prime of his fighting career, Tiger met a challenger he just couldn't defeat. Like so many cats given free rein to roam unattended, Tiger ended his life beneath the wheels of some passing vehicle on the street in front of the tiny kingdom he had ruled over for so long.

We were never certain of what exactly had drawn him out into traffic. He had been content

**LEFT** *Nearly all cats like to keep an eye on other cats in the neighbourhood to ensure that the accepted territorial rules are being observed.*

**LEFT** *For the cat who is allowed outdoors, regular patrols of the territory are quickly turned into ritual behaviour that must be followed on every outing.*

## CAT WATCHING TIP

You may not think your cat has a territory, but all cats do in some form. Follow your cat out into the garden. Make note of where it goes, what it looks at, what it marks, and how it reacts to other creatures in its proximity. Notice where it settles down and what paths it takes to get to where it wants to be. Note if there is also a common ground where it meets up with other cats, and what kind of social standing your cat seems to have as a member of the group. Do this for several days because the cat might not cover all its territory in just one.

to remain more or less within his territory prior to that fatal exception. Our buildings, fences, hedgerows and such had always seemed to suit him just fine for the boundaries of his domain.

Perhaps he had caught the scent of some female elsewhere in the neighbourhood or had found something objectionable about the food we had offered him that day. Except for those individual cats who are best described as having the wanderlust in their blood, mating and food are about the only things that will draw a cat from well-established territory.

Cats are perfectly happy to accept our man-made structures and contrivances as the boundaries to their territories, but not because they are following any direction on our part. No territory can be adequate, in the cat's opinion, unless it provides safe and secure places to sleep, eat and drink, relieve oneself, and play. And, in general, each of these places should be somewhat removed from all of the others. Even the cat that never gets beyond the confines of the house wants things this way. A litter box placed too close to the food bowl, therefore, may be the answer to a suddenly finicky cat.

## ESTABLISHING TERRITORY

Territory size varies from one cat to the next and from one terrain to another. A cat in a small city apartment may claim only a couple of dozen square feet. A feral cat, living off the rodents and food scraps it can find in the streets, alleys and vacant buildings, may nightly roam many city blocks. A cat living on a farm in an isolated rural setting may lord over many, many acres.

Where the territories of two cats meet, there will generally be a small buffer zone of shared ground. We humans won't recognize this zone, but the cats have mutually agreed that they both may use this area for moving from one section of

**ABOVE** *An intruder brazenly breaks the territorial barrier, encroaching on the realm of a fellow feline who isn't able to fend off the assault just now.*

**RIGHT** *Territorial behaviour can be displayed toward non-cat species as well. Dogs are a particular target, but even humans can be told in no uncertain terms that they are trespassing.*

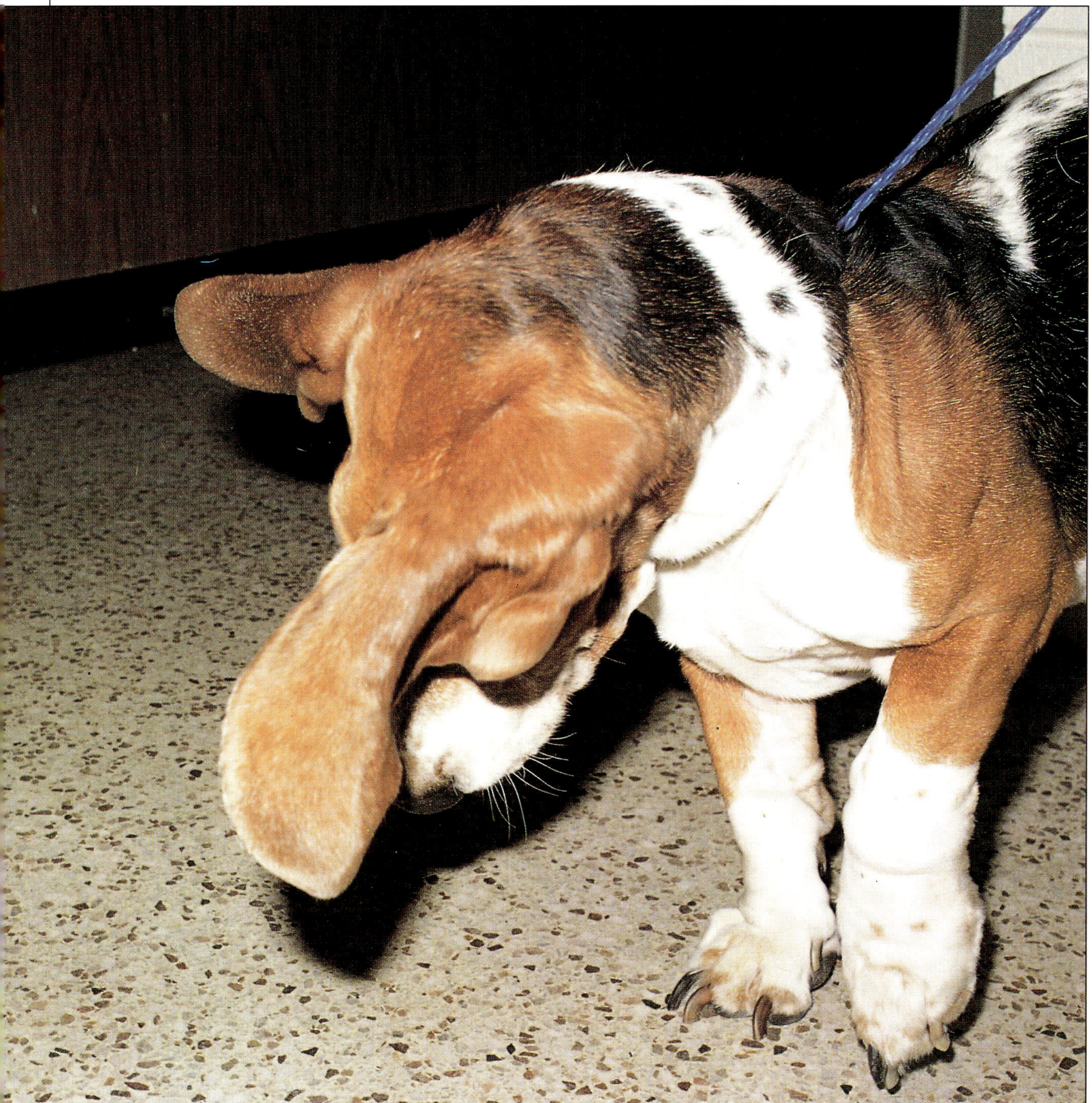

territory to the next or for hunting (only at different times).

A section of common ground is best described as the town hall. On this spot, which is claimed by no individual, the felines gather occasionally. Mating is often not the reason for their gatherings, as you might expect at first. Exactly what is "discussed" and "decided" has not yet been revealed to any human. These occasional gatherings do not negate our comments elsewhere in the book that cats are a good deal less social than many other creatures.

Ancestral instinct accounts for all this territorial behaviour. It comes down to our domestic cats from their forbears, who lived in the wild and fought every day for their continued existence.

# Territorial Rules

The extent of a cat's territory depends on its position in the hierarchy. Queens with kittens (far right) have small territories which they defend fiercely. A tom (left) will probably have the most extensive area. All cats will avoid gardens where there is a dog, but some areas, such as paths, will be communal.

To those animals, the scent of food or their own waste too close to their sleeping area would certainly reveal their location to predators. In addition, the scents they left about their territory – both in their wastes and in glandular secretions – would warn off potential intruders of their own kind, who would otherwise compete with them for the essentials of life.

In the descendants of these wild ancestors the instinct still remains to claw the furniture like unleashed demons. How else will any intruding cats that happen along know that they are trespassing on someone else's territory?

Although nearly every cat needs some time to himself at regular intervals, those that share a house or garden with other cats may come to see that area as a jointly owned territory. In something akin to the much stronger pack behaviour in dogs, these cats will join together in the defence of their territory against all intruders.

An adaptation on this shared-territory scenario is a shift-work scheme in which the different cats actually take responsibility for guarding their grounds at different times. The other members of this "pack" will be found resting, eating, drinking or playing.